#MILLENNIALtweet

140 Bite-sized Ideas for Managing the Millennials

By Alexandra Levit
Foreword by Lisa Orrell

First Printing: September 2009

Paperback ISBN: 978-1-60773-058-3
Place of Publication: Silicon Valley, California USA

Paperback Library of Congress Number: 2009936459

eBook ISBN: 978-1-60773-059-0

Advance Praise
(in alphabetical order)

"Alexandra gives awesome advice in this quick guide to help engage Millennial employees and bridge the digital divide."

Lance Haun @thelance, Blogger, Your HR Guy

"Alexandra Levit is one of the few experts who understands how to work with twenty-somethings. This book belongs on every manager's desk!"

Monica O'Brien @monicaobrien, Twenty-something Marketing Expert

---

"'#MILLENNIALtweet' is well-crafted and wise. Levit understands Millennials. Like tapas, this creative book makes a tasty, satisfying meal."

Carol Phillips @carol_phillips, Founder of Brand Amplitude

"An expert on workplace issues, Levit writes a book on managing Millennials that's fun, packed with practical ideas, and even inspiring."

Steven Rothberg @stevenrothberg, Founder of CollegeRecruiter.com

---

"'#MILLENNIALtweet' will give you the skills and traits to manage, inspire, and shape your Millennial workforce into the leaders of tomorrow."

Laurie Ruettimann @lruettimann, Blogger, Punk Rock HR

Acknowledgments

Jason Alba *@JasonAlba* for helping me to see where I wanted to go.

Mitchell Levy *@HappyAbout* for providing the guidebook.

Rajesh Setty *@UpbeatNow* for allowing me a seat on his train.

Lisa Orrell *@GenerationsGuru*, Carol Phillips *@carol_phillips*, Monica O'Brien *@monicaobrien*, Laurie Ruettimann *@lruettimann*, Steven Rothberg *@stevenrothberg*, and Lance Haun *@thelance* for their advance reads and support.

Why I wrote this book?

To provide all the info you need about recruiting, managing, and retaining Millennials—in the duration of one short plane ride!

Alexandra Levit *@alevit*

Contents

Foreword by Lisa Orrell

"Alexandra Levit has created an amazing resource guide, in Tweet-sized bites, for engaging Millennial talent. A must read for employers!"

Lisa Orrell @ *GenerationsGuru*, Author of Millennials Incorporated

Section 1

Millennials in Context

Learn about the Millennials' place in the inter-generational pool that is your organization.

1

It's a chorus heard all over today's business world: "Who hired those Millennials and what can I do about them?"

2

Managers lament: "I don't understand. I get along great with my 22-year-old daughter, but my same-aged employee is impossible!"

3

The Millennials, or the young professionals causing the uproar, are the youngest of the four generations currently in the workforce.

4

The Traditionalists: Born before 1946, they're the loyalists who spent a lifetime at the company and want that gold watch.

5

Baby Boomers: Born 1946–64, they're the hippies and the yuppies who worshipped the Beatles and clawed their way to the top.

6

Generation X: Born 1965–77, they're the loners who learned to be self-reliant when their parents left them with latchkeys.

7

Millennials: Born after 1978 (some say 1980), they're the techies whose parents taught them they were special and entitled.

8

Not all age-related stereotypes are false. If you listen to people in your office, you can hear clear differences in the way they talk.

9

Traditionalists might say: "How can I help YOU? Flexibility is a code word for less work getting done. If I'm not yelling at you, you're doing fine."

10

Baby Boomers: "I paid my dues to get more money. We're doing something right to be in business this long. Get your feedback at the review."

11

Gen X-ers: "Company loyalty—what's that? I can manage my own career, thank you very much. Give me the skills or give me death."

12

Millennials: "Sorry to interrupt, but you haven't told me how I'm doing today. Let's cut out the red tape, okay? How can YOU help ME?"

13

The Millennials are the largest generation in history, with 80 million members in the US. They surpass the Boomers and dwarf Gen X!

14

Starting with the Boomers' retirement, the Millennials will be asked to take on leadership roles at a younger age.

15

Top food manufacturer: "In 2008, the average age of our engineers was 57, and by 2015, it will be 27. How's that for a transfer of power?"

Section II

Millennials in the World

Besides being large, the Millennial generation attracts attention because of their unprecedented attitudes.

16

Many say Millennials are the same as the previous 20-somethings, and clashes occur because younger workers always annoy older workers.

17

But Millennials bring with them a variety of unique life experiences and perspectives that will shape the workplace of the 21st century.

18

Let's start with diversity. Millennials think it's weird that companies spend so much money on these programs. They take diversity for granted.

19

10% of Millennials have a non-citizen parent, and 17% speak a language besides English at home. 60% have dated someone of a different race.

20

Thanks to the global web, Millennials have routinely interacted with other cultures for most of their lives, and are comfortable doing it.

21

Raised by indulgent parents who nurtured their self-esteem, Millennials are ready to overcome challenges and leap tall buildings.

22

Millennials consider their parents as role models. A huge majority has close relationships with both parents.

23

While parents of Gen X-ers were lucky if their kids called from college once a week, most Millennials talk to their parents every day!

24

If you think about what has shaped Millennial perceptions of the world, it's terrorism, heroism, and technology.

25

Oklahoma City, Columbine, and 9/11 all occurred during childhood. The concept of "hero" returned to popular consciousness with 9/11.

26

Millennials are looking for heroes at work, including executives and managers who inspire them to do their best and make a difference.

27

Millennials live on their devices, getting their news from blogs and texting and IM'ing on a minute-by-minute basis.

28

Millennials grew up with technology that allowed for instant gratification—information they wanted, how and when they wanted it.

29

In the Millennial mind, there is no "right" way to do something. They want to customize everything to suit their needs!

30

Managers who want Millennials to put down their phones and focus on one task at a time are going to lose that battle.

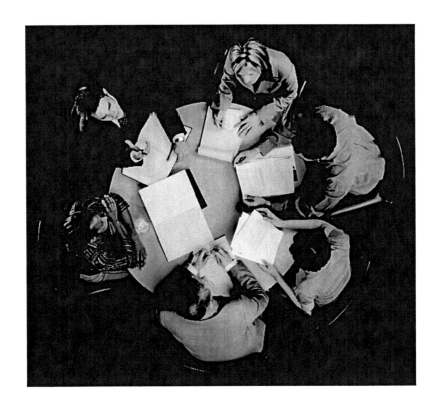

Section III

Millennials at Work

Millennials aren't the meek and deferential young professionals of yesteryear. They're ready to dive in!

31

The recent economic downturn has caused Millennials in the workplace to adjust their expectations and become more self-aware.

32

Millennials graduating college today are significantly less arrogant and entitled than their older brothers and sisters.

33

Long-term payoffs don't cut it. They want to know what you can do for them today.

34

Even as entry-level employees, Millennials want a job to fit into their lives, not the other way around.

35

They strive to be entrepreneurial, even in the context of Corporate America. They want the chance to innovate and solve problems.

36

Millennials aren't interested in paying their dues or making sacrifices for the organization.

37

While some Millennials think they could do a good job running your company, most just want the opportunity to do meaningful work.

38

Millennials appreciate the apprentice mode of learning. They will watch superiors carefully and then put their own spin on it.

39

Millennials don't care about hierarchy. If they disagree with a policy, they'll tell anyone who will listen.

40

Millennials don't perceive a gulf between themselves and their managers. Everyone is equal; bosses are just older.

41

Millennials thrive on collaboration. They want to work closely with their managers and team members.

42

Like their older Generation X siblings, Millennials value skill acquisition over a predictable career path.

43

Young professionals want constructive feedback in real time. Constructive = respectful delivery, helpful content.

44

Millennials multi-task extremely
well and soak up knowledge
quickly, often making up for
a lack of experience.

45

They relish responsibility and want
to own projects completely, whether
you think they're ready or not.

46

Millennials are comfortable with change. They expect mobility, inside and outside their current organization.

47

Millennials can be very loyal once you have demonstrated that you deserve their loyalty.

Section IV

Millennials' Ideal Organization

Millennials know where they want to work and are looking for a perfect fit, not just a perfect job.

48

The organization is customer-focused and has a mission that Millennials can believe in.

49

The organization provides a competitive salary, and also important benefits like health coverage and retirement contributions.

50

The organization offers top-notch training and mentoring opportunities to grow their skill base and do their jobs better.

51

The organization has a fun and collegial culture where members of the different generations communicate seamlessly.

52

The organization has global relationships and understands different cultures, and provides the potential to work overseas.

53

The organization is naturally inclusive. When they walk into the lobby, Millennials see all types of people.

54

The organization is socially responsible. It makes good products and services and gives back to the community.

55

The organization offers structured volunteer opportunities that Millennials can take advantage of, on and off the job.

56

The organization balances a cutting-edge use of technology with more traditional people interaction.

57

The organization recognizes the value that young professionals bring to the table and gives credit where credit is due.

58

The organization maintains a culture in which leaders are receptive to employee input and act quickly to fix problems.

59

The organization encourages employee innovation and has processes in place for "intrapreneurship."

60

The organization is supportive
of the Millennial desire
to balance work with family,
friends, and hobbies.

61

The organization has already
set a precedent for employing
flexible work options such as
telecommuting and job sharing.

Section V

Recruiting the Best and the Brightest

Even in a tough economy, it's up to you to seek out leadership-worthy candidates.

62

If you're going to recruit at colleges, send your best people to represent the company. Millennials are paying attention.

63

Consider reaching out to underclassmen so you can develop deep relationships well before graduation.

64

Find Millennial gems by keeping close contact with nearby colleges and nonprofit organizations that cater to young professionals.

65

Enlist the highest performing Millennials to recruit their friends, and reward them for doing so.

66

If a job isn't glamorous, don't lie about it. They'll figure it out eventually, will quit, and will then badmouth you.

67

On a related note, tell them about your unique training and volunteer programs, but be prepared to deliver what you promise.

68

Millennials expect an intuitive and efficient company website and want to fill out information online.

69

Millennials use the Internet to seek out opinions, so monitor what's being said about you on social networks and blogs.

70

Have an up-to-date presence where the Millennial job hunters are: Facebook, YouTube, LinkedIn, Twitter, and sites like CareerTV.com.

71

Did you read sections III and IV? Update those stale recruiting materials to reflect the current twenty-something values.

72

Conduct initial phone screenings with all Millennial candidates to ensure they're worthy of an office visit.

73

Show personal interest in each Millennial candidate. Provide information quickly and keep all prospective hires in the loop.

74

Use behavior-based
questioning and work
simulations to assess
whether a candidate is
a strong fit
for the position.

75

Identify the skills and traits most critical for Millennial hires and consider designing an assessment to probe for those.

76

Give them a better picture of the job by hooking them up with a satisfied employee their age who can address questions and concerns.

77

Millennials are not big fans of risk. Don't hire someone who just wants a job because he/she can't stand to be unemployed.

78

Hasten the hiring process as much as you can. Millennials have little patience for bureaucratic delays.

79

Case study: Millennial recruits found Deloitte employee films transparent, authentic, and personally meaningful.

80

For more on recruitment best practices, please see the book, Success for Hire: Simple Strategies to Find and Keep Outstanding Employees.

Section VI

Bringing Them on Painlessly

Millennials form their impressions very quickly. Here's how not to let them down.

81

Get started on the right foot. Communicate actively with Millennial hires between the offer and start dates.

82

Make sure someone on your team is on top of what will happen on their first day. Don't rest on HR's laurels.

83

An engaging orientation is important, but it's not everything. Have their business cards, cubicle, and first project ready.

84

Take new hires out to lunch and inquire about their dreams and aspirations, showing you care about their growth and success.

85

If you're the immediate supervisor, state your expectations upfront (for example, how you'd like to receive work updates).

86

Millennials want
to be challenged
right away, so trust
them with individual
components of
your most
significant projects.

87

Explain why your company does tasks a certain way, and how their jobs fit into the big picture of the organization's mission.

88

Make sure Millennials understand what a good work ethic looks like in your workplace, but be flexible in how they get their jobs done.

89

Teach them how to adapt to the workplace culture. Educate them on the ins and outs of your business (written and unwritten rules, etc.).

90

Show Millennials the "work arounds" you've learned for getting things done quickly in the organization.

91

Spell out how they should prepare and conduct themselves in meetings with other departments, senior executives, or clients.

92

Guide them in networking around the company. Facilitate coaching opportunities with star employees who are experts in various areas.

93

Demonstrate how you organize your work flow—for example, via to-do lists and Google documents.

94

Set Millennials up with project management software to help them estimate time and resources accurately.

95

Schedule one-on-one meetings with young employees once a week to provide a sense of structure as well as ongoing guidance and support.

Section VII

Best Practices for Millennial Management

The best Millennial supervisor is an active and collaborative supervisor.

96

Direct their energy into assignments that will keep them on the right side of the law while giving them genuine decision-making power.

97

Ask for their input on the work they're assigned and how that work should best be completed.

98

Encourage Millennials to incorporate learning into their jobs and to express their ideas for improving the organization's work.

99

You are not their parents, so don't hover or micromanage. Set project goals and let them be creative within certain boundaries.

100

Millennials want you to help them gain transferable skills that will be useful throughout their careers.

101

Help them
practice assertive
communication and
good writing,
speaking, and
listening techniques.

102

The good news is Millennials can multi-task very well. The bad news is they have short attention spans and lose track of details.

103

Teach them to organize their schedule around their most important tasks and break down complex projects into digestible chunks.

104

If you're a direct supervisor, help them prioritize assignments and run interference with colleagues competing for their time.

105

Allow them to work by your side during a crisis so that they can learn good judgment and systematic problem solving.

106

Encourage Millennials to take ownership of issues, especially when customer problems fall in their laps.

107

Model the notion of treating everyone like a VIP. Assistants are often more useful to Millennial employees than their bosses.

108

Be straightforward about the importance of "playing well in the sandbox"—and practice what you preach.

109

Provide frequent, consistent, and constructive feedback. Don't wait for review time to tell Millennials how they're doing.

110

When delivering feedback, don't harp on the negative, but accentuate the positive where you can. Focus on one issue at a time!

111

Millennials tend to live in the here and now. When a contribution is made, give private and/or public recognition right away.

112

Reward high-performing Millennials with small bonuses and other perks like comp days and happy hours.

113

Promote work/life balance by helping Millennial employees to balance your requirements with their other commitments.

114

If you think there's a star in your midst, do whatever you can to keep him/her—even if it's facilitating an internal move.

115

Watch for burnout among your top performers and redesign jobs that are exhausting, boring, or repetitive.

116

Anticipate staffing needs ahead of time and make sure ongoing training allows Millennials to do their jobs efficiently and well.

117

Recruit your most talented Millennials to serve as mentors for new college hires.

118

Collect feedback from Millennials, both directly and anonymously (360 degree reviews, surveys, etc.), and take their thoughts seriously.

119

Beware of the mindset that you want all Millennials to stay. Put poor performers on probation.

120

Case study: Campbell's Soup engaged Millennials by allowing young employees to share their views at a global leadership meeting.

Section VIII

Engage Them Using
Social Media

Understand and participate in
Millennial culture with trips to their
virtual worlds.

121

Since you're currently reading this, you're ahead of other people who still think social media is just a kid's thing.

122

At the end of 2008, there were 100 million videos on YouTube, 200 million blogs, and 100 million Facebook users.

123

As Brian Solis said in the Social Media Manifesto, if you're not on a social networking site, you might as well not be online.

124

In a new community, pay attention to how things are done and the buzz about your industry and organization.

125

Millennials are googling you, so make sure that you're well represented in internal and external search engines.

126

Think about where to draw the line in terms of who can view your content on the various social networks.

127

For example, you might use Facebook personally and LinkedIn professionally. Avoid hurt feelings by explaining your logic.

128

Don't "friend blast"—it's quality, not quantity. Send personalized notes indicating why you're interested in someone.

129

Millennials are prickly about employers using social networks to do background checks. If you must, do it on the down low.

130

Distribute communications and company news via text messages and RSS (really simple syndication).

131

Save yourself event planning headaches and expenses by putting your training on podcasts they can listen to, on the way to work.

132

Millennials won't open your e-newsletter or visit your flat Intranet content. Try a blog that allows anonymous commenting.

133

Coordinate online forums for Millennials to express ideas about the organization. Address criticism and respond to suggestions.

134

Create brainstorm, knowledge sharing, and expertise wikis so Millennials can take ownership of projects.

135

Remember that online communication should be a dialogue, not a monologue. You can't control every word, and that's okay.

136

Encourage your Millennials to follow and appropriately converse with senior team members and executives on Twitter.

137

Before spending any money on social media, take a walk down to your IT department to see what's already in place.

138

Social media engagement is often the perfect project to engage Millennial hires. Get their help on what to do and how to do it.

139

Millennials are light years ahead when it comes to new technologies. Find out what they want to use and invest in getting it for them.

140

Case study: Microsoft made a major employee announcement via a viral video sketch. The result? Hundreds of thousands of downloads!

Afterword

Millennials are
empowered and driven
to change businesses
for the better. Getting
them in your corner is
the key to 21st century
competitiveness.

140 Bite-sized Ideas for Managing the Millennials

About the Author

Alexandra Levit is a nationally recognized business and workplace expert and the author of the bestselling *They Don't Teach Corporate in College* and *New Job, New You*. Known as one of the premiere spokespeople of her generation, Alexandra regularly speaks at conferences, universities, and corporations including Campbell's Soup, CIGNA, the Federal Reserve Bank, McDonalds, and Whirlpool—on issues facing modern employees. Alexandra is also a member of the Business Roundtable's Springboard Project, which is advising the Obama administration on current workplace challenges. Find her on Twitter @alevit.

LaVergne, TN USA
18 October 2009
161167LV00002BA/2/P